OFFICE OF INSPECTOR GENERAL
Department of Homeland Security

Washington, DC 20528 / www.oig.dhs.gov

I0410763

September 12, 2013

MEMORANDUM FOR: Thomas S. Winkowski
                  Deputy Commissioner
                  Performing the duties of the Commissioner of CBP
                  U.S. Customs and Border Protection

FROM: Charles K. Edwards
                  Deputy Inspector General

SUBJECT: *CBP Use of Force Training and Actions To Address Use of Force Incidents – Redacted (Revised)*

Attached for your action is our revised final report, *CBP Use of Force Training and Actions To Address Use of Force Incidents – Redacted (Revised), OIG-13-114.* We incorporated the formal comments from U.S. Customs and Border Protection in the final report. This revised version is redacted due to deliberative material.

The report contains three recommendations aimed at improving the U.S. Customs and Border Protection Office of Training and Development and the Office of Internal Affairs. Your office concurred with all of the recommendations. Based on information provided in your response to the draft report, we consider the three recommendations resolved. Once your office has fully implemented each recommendation, please submit a formal closeout letter to us within 30 days so that we may close the recommendation. The memorandum should be accompanied by evidence of completion of agreed-upon corrective actions.

Please email a signed PDF copy of all responses and closeout requests to OIGInspectionsFollowup@oig.dhs.gov.

Consistent with our responsibility under the *Inspector General Act*, we are providing copies of our report to appropriate congressional committees with oversight and appropriation responsibility over the Department of Homeland Security. We will post a redacted version of the report on our website.

Please call me with any questions, or your staff may contact Deborah Outten-Mills, Acting Assistant Inspector General for Inspections, at (202) 254-4015.

Attachment

Table of Contents

Appendixes

Abbreviations

CBP	U.S. Customs and Border Protection
DHS	Department of Homeland Security
EDS	Enterprise Data System
FY	fiscal year
ICE	U.S. Immigration and Customs Enforcement
JICMS	Joint Intake Case Management System
OAM	Office of Air and Marine
OBP	Office of Border Patrol
OFO	Office of Field Operations
OIA	Office of Internal Affairs

OIG	Office of Inspector General
OPR	Office of Professional Responsibility
OTD	Office of Training and Development
PBS	Public Broadcasting Service
PERF	Police Executive Research Forum
UFPD	Use of Force Policy Division
UFRS	Use of Force Reporting System

Executive Summary

Following April 2012 media reports regarding the death of an undocumented immigrant while in the custody of U.S. Customs and Border Protection (CBP) in May 2010, Senator Robert Menendez and 15 members of Congress requested that we review the use of force within CBP. We reviewed allegations of the use of excessive force by CBP employees and determined what reforms CBP has implemented. We also examined what effect adding more agents and officers to the workforce has had on training and professionalism.

Allegations of employee misconduct that are entered into Department of Homeland Security (DHS) case management systems are assigned one of several case allegation types; however, there is no primary use of force designation. As a result, we were unable to identify the total number of excessive force allegations and investigations involving CBP employees.

The August 2006 to December 2009 workforce surge within CBP did not negatively affect use of force training within CBP. Use of force training remained consistent and funding for use of force training increased at the basic training academies. Pre employment polygraph examinations have improved the quality of the CBP workforce.

CBP has taken several steps to address the number of use of force incidents involving CBP employees and to ensure that agents and officers use force only when necessary and reasonable. All CBP law enforcement agents and officers are required to follow the same use of force policy and standards and complete the same use of force training. CBP tracks all use of force incidents and recently completed an internal review of use of force issues.

However, more can be done. The CBP Office of Training and Development Use of Force Policy Division should incorporate additional assault data into its analysis of use of force incidents and formalize and expand its field audit program. CBP should continue to expand the use of scenario based training and assess new technologies to support agents and officers.

We are making three recommendations. CBP should work with U.S. Immigration and Customs Enforcement (ICE) to implement a method to identify excessive force allegations in its case management system, develop processes to incorporate information regarding assaults on agents that do not result in the use of force into its analysis of use of force incidents, and evaluate and act upon field audit results. The DHS Office of Inspector General (OIG) will modify its case management system to identify in greater detail incidents involving excessive use of force allegations.

Background

In April 2012, the Public Broadcasting Service (PBS) aired a report regarding the death of a person while in the custody of CBP in May 2010. This incident and others raised concerns regarding use of force training and accountability within DHS and CBP. U.S. Senator Robert Menendez and 15 members of Congress requested that we review the use of force within CBP.

Use of Force

CBP's policies and procedures for use of force describe the amount of force that is reasonable and necessary for a law enforcement agent or officer to use when compelling an unwilling subject to comply with lawful commands. Reasonable means there are objective reasons that justify the level of force used in a given situation, up to and including deadly force. Necessary means that some force is required in the situation to carry out law enforcement duties. Force would be deemed excessive if it were later determined to have been either unnecessary or unreasonably forceful.

The CBP Use of Force Continuum describes the levels of force an agent or officer may need to use to gain control over a subject. At the lowest level on the continuum, officer presence and spoken commands are sufficient when a subject is cooperative. If a subject does not comply with spoken commands or is passively resisting, the agent or officer may need to use physical contact techniques, such as strategic positioning or pressure point stimulation, to gain compliance. If a subject actively resists an agent's efforts to gain control or assaults or displays a willingness to assault an agent or officer, the agent or officer would use escalating, less lethal force options to compel compliance. For example, agents and officers could use oleoresin capsicum (pepper spray) or an electronic control device, or taser, against an actively resistant subject and could also use a collapsible straight baton (baton) if the subject becomes assaultive. An agent or officer is authorized to use the highest level, deadly force, only when the agent or officer believes the subject poses an imminent danger of death or serious physical injury to the agent or officer or another person, and the subject has the opportunity, ability, and intent to do so.

In determining the appropriate level of force, CBP trains its law enforcement officers to consider the totality of the circumstances in each situation. This training includes: the level of training, mental attitude, strength, age, and size of the officer; size of the subject; the subject's actions; weapons involved; presence of other officers; number of subjects present; bystanders; and environmental conditions. Generally, the officer should use the lowest level of force necessary to control the situation. Because of unique circumstances and individual differences in every potential confrontation, different officers might have different responses to the same situation, all of which may be reasonable and necessary.

Rapid Surge of CBP Workforce

In May 2006, the President mandated that CBP add 6,000 new Border Patrol Agents by December 2008. CBP increased the number of Border Patrol Agents by more than 50 percent from August 2006 through December 2009 (see table 1). During the same time period, the number of CBP officers also increased.

Table 1: Number of Border Patrol Agents and CBP Officers FY 2006–FY 2012

Fiscal Year	Total OBP	Total OFO	Total CBP
2006	12,349	17,733	30,082
2007	14,923	18,272	33,195
2008	17,499	19,568	37,067
2009	20,119	21,103	41,222
2010	20,558	20,455	41,013
2011	21,444	20,379	41,823
2012	21,394	21,790	43,184

Source: CBP Office of Border Patrol (OBP) and Office of Field Operations (OFO).

As the number of agents and officers increased, the number of supervisory agents and officers also increased proportionately. Within the Office of Border Patrol (OBP), supervisory agents accounted for 17 percent of all agents from fiscal year (FY) 2006–FY 2007, 18 percent from FY 2008–FY 2009, and 19 percent from FY 2010–FY 2012. Within the Office of Field Operations (OFO), supervisory officers accounted for 13 percent of all officers from FY 2006–FY 2011 and 14 percent in FY 2012.

Operational Environment

CBP agents and officers operate in a variety of border environments and conditions. CBP officers operate at land, air, and sea ports of entry, which are largely controlled environments due to designated lanes and processing areas. CBP officers generally work in teams or in close proximity to other officers, with backup readily available should it be needed. Border Patrol Agents operate between ports of entry along U.S. borders. The terrain along U.S. borders varies greatly, ranging from dense forests and open plains along the northern border to open deserts, rugged mountains, the Rio Grande River, and coastal waters along the southern border. Border Patrol Agents often patrol alone; the nearest agent could be 10 to 20 miles away.

DHS has completed the construction of more than 600 miles of fencing and has installed surveillance technology to detect and inhibit illegal border crossings into the United States. This has limited the areas along the southwest border where illegal border crossers attempt to enter the United States and has increased the chance they will be intercepted by the Border Patrol. Violent assaults against Border Patrol Agents rose to a peak in 2010, and have diminished since then.

CBP began tracking assaults on Border Patrol Agents in 2006. Assault information is reported in the Assault Module of the CBP e3 system. The e3 system is used to record, transmit, and retrieve information for CBP enforcement purposes, such as biographic and property information. The system also captures or verifies biometric information of apprehended individuals.

From FY 2006 to FY 2012, 99 percent of assaults on Border Patrol Agents occurred along the southwest border of the United States (see table 2).

Table 2: Assaults on Border Patrol Agents, FY 2006–FY 2012

Fiscal Year	Southwest Border	Northern Border	Coastal Border	Total
2006	729	16	7	752
2007	979	6	2	987
2008	1,085	10	2	1,097
2009	1,031	11	6	1,048
2010	1,050	10	2	1,062
2011	678	2	7	687
2012	543	6	0	549
Total	6,095	61	26	6,182

Source: CBP Office of Border Patrol.

Results of Review

Information regarding complaints of employee misconduct, and any subsequent investigative activity, is tracked and maintained in case management systems. Although these systems include a data field that assigns specific types of misconduct, such as excessive force, discrimination, abuse of authority, and other categories, to a primary allegation type, there is no primary use of force allegation designation. As a result, we were unable to determine the total number of excessive force allegations and investigations involving CBP employees.

We determined that use of force training before and during the workforce surge remained consistent. Funding at the basic training academies increased in proportion to the increase in trainees. The implementation of polygraph examinations for all prospective law enforcement agents and officers prior to being hired has improved the quality of the CBP workforce by detecting unsuitable candidates who might otherwise have been selected.

To address use of force incidents involving CBP employees and to ensure that agents and officers use force only when necessary and reasonable, CBP has (1) completed an internal review of use of force issues; (2) begun tracking all use of force incidents; (3) improved consistency in training for agents and officers, and the application of use of force standards and policies; (4) initiated a field audit program to evaluate use of force training across CBP field locations; and (5) commissioned an independent review of use of force by the Police Executive Research Forum (PERF).

Excessive Use of Force Allegations and Investigations Were Not Identified in Case Management Systems

The DHS OIG Hotline and the Joint Intake Center receive complaints about employee misconduct that include allegations of excessive force, discrimination, off duty arrests, abuse of authority, and others. We attempted to obtain information that would enable us to analyze and summarize excessive force investigations involving CBP employees. Allegations entered into DHS case management systems are assigned one of several case allegation types; however, there is no primary use of force designation. As a result, we were unable to identify the total number of excessive use of force allegations and investigations involving CBP employees.

Documenting Allegations of Excessive Force

The OIG Hotline and the Joint Intake Center, operated by CBP and ICE, receive allegations of misconduct by DHS employees, including allegations that CBP employees have used excessive force. Hotline and Center staff enter the details into their respective case management system—the Enterprise Data System (EDS) or the Joint Intake Case Management System (JICMS).

No matter to which of the two offices the allegation was addressed, the OIG Office of Investigations first has the option to investigate or decline to investigate an allegation. If OIG declines, the ICE Office of Professional Responsibility (OPR) and then the CBP Office of Internal Affairs (OIA), respectively, decide whether to investigate. Many allegations are determined to be administrative—non criminal misbehavior—and are referred to management for action.

Each allegation is assigned to a primary category; however, neither case management system has a primary category that designates an allegation as use of force. In JICMS, excessive use of force allegations are assigned to primary categories to include detainee/alien (physical abuse), detainee/alien abuse (other), detainee/alien abuse (medical issue), and death detainee/alien/civilian (result of agency action). In EDS, primary categories for use of force allegations include civil rights/civil liberties or miscellaneous. In addition to a primary category, OIG also identifies a secondary type of allegation. While one secondary allegation type is "use of force," and includes some excessive force allegations, other excessive force allegations are designated as detainee /prisoner /suspect related abuse, criminal misconduct, or non criminal misconduct. In addition, we identified allegations that were placed improperly in the secondary use of force allegation type.

To determine the universe of excessive force investigations involving CBP employees, we received data sets from OIG and JICMS that included more than 21,000 records of possible excessive force allegations. Because excessive force allegations are assigned to multiple categories, the narrative in each allegation summary must be reviewed to determine whether it was an excessive use of force allegation.

Of the more than 21,000 records that we received, we reviewed the allegation summary field for the 2,093 records from JICMS data—excessive force and abuse allegations and intentional discharge of weapon. This included 1,896 records from FYs 2007 through 2012 in the excessive force and abuse data. We identified 1,187 of these records as possible allegations related to excessive force (see figure 1). The allegations also included physical abuse (punching, kicking, and pushing) during apprehension, and use of an electronic control device, baton, or pepper spray.

We identified 205 records as not being excessive force allegations, such as claims of improper detention, racial profiling, and initial allegations that were later recanted. For 504 records, we were unable to conclude that they were excessive use of force allegations based on information in the allegation summary field. Types of information in these summary fields included alleged civil rights violations and physical abuse.

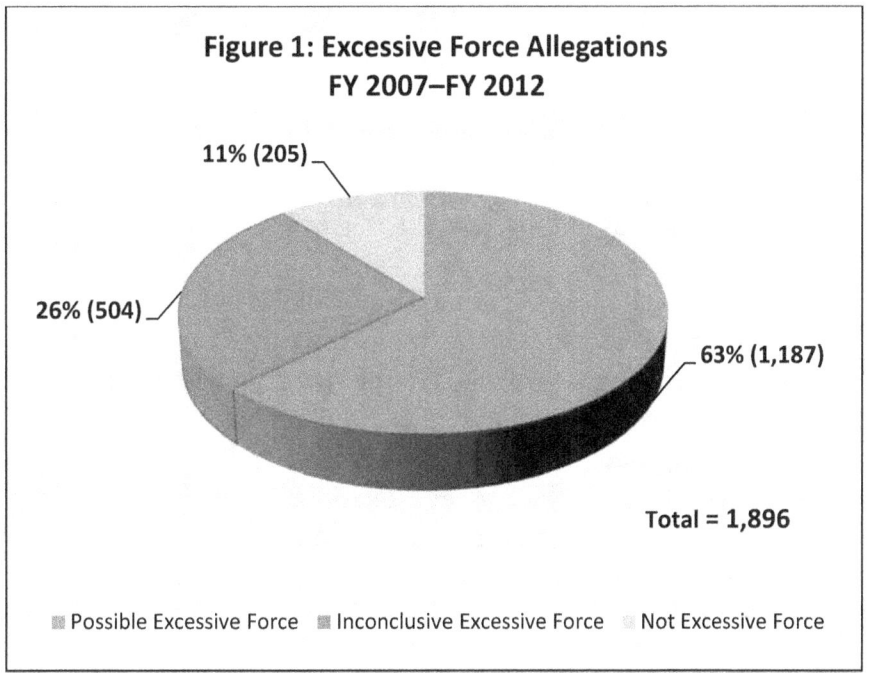

Figure 1: Excessive Force Allegations FY 2007–FY 2012

11% (205)

26% (504)

63% (1,187)

Total = 1,896

▪ Possible Excessive Force ▪ Inconclusive Excessive Force ▪ Not Excessive Force

Source: CBP Office of Internal Affairs, JICMS.

We also reviewed the allegation summary field of 197 records from FY 2009–FY 2012 for intentional discharge of weapon data, and identified 136 possible use of force incidents involving the discharge of a weapon (see figure 2). We were not able to determine whether 39 of these records were use of force incidents and concluded that 22 were not use of force incidents.

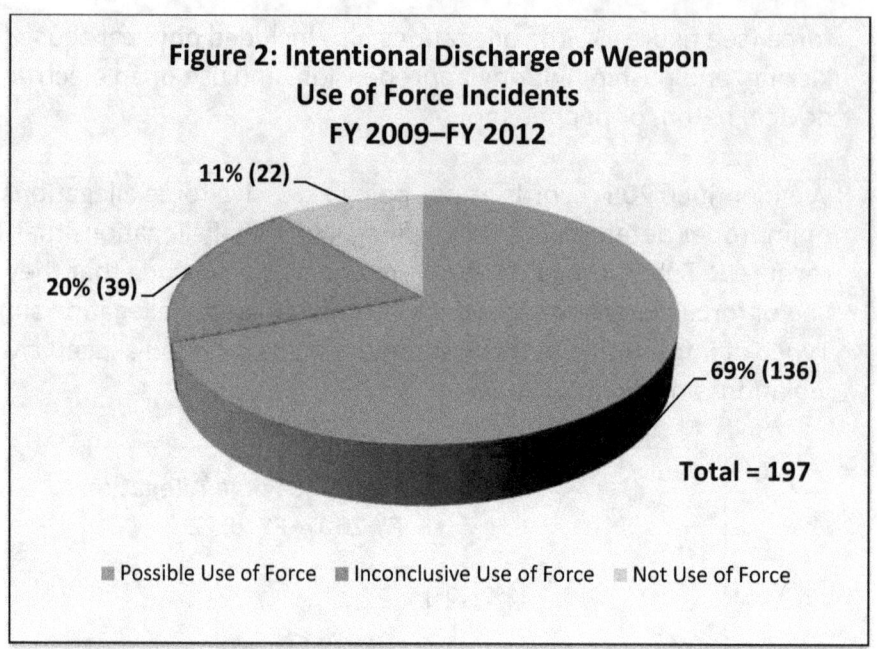

Figure 2: Intentional Discharge of Weapon Use of Force Incidents FY 2009–FY 2012

11% (22)

20% (39)

69% (136)

Total = 197

Possible Use of Force   Inconclusive Use of Force   Not Use of Force

Source: CBP Office of Internal Affairs, JICMS.

CBP OIA officials suggested that a new field to indicate whether an allegation involves use of force should be added to JICMS. However, JICMS is an ICE computer system. CBP officials raised the issue with ICE in April 2013 and told us that they are continuing to work with ICE to develop an indicator. We concur with the proposed addition of a use of force indicator field to JICMS. Also, we have asked the OIG Office of Investigations to modify its case management system to identify in greater detail incidents involving use of force allegations. The OIG Office of Investigations will do so.

Recommendation

We recommend that U.S. Customs and Border Protection:

Recommendation #1:

Work with ICE to implement a method in JICMS to identify each use of force allegation involving an officer or agent.

Workforce Surge Did Not Affect Use of Force Training

The August 2006 to December 2009 workforce surge within CBP did not negatively affect use of force training within CBP. Use of force training content and hours remained consistent, and funding for use of force training increased at the basic academies. Since October 2010, all CBP law enforcement agents and officers receive quarterly firearms and less lethal device training.

Use of Force Training at Basic Academies

Agents and officers receive use of force training as part of their basic academy training to become Border Patrol Agents or CBP officers. Use of force training at the basic academies includes instruction in firearms proficiency and judgment shooting, threat assessment and response, the use of force continuum, use of force legal authorities, physical techniques, baton certification, and pepper spray certification. Since 2010, CBP officer trainees also complete taser certification during basic training.

Use of force training at both basic training academies remained consistent throughout the workforce surge. While the number of trainees entering the basic academies increased in FY 2007, FY 2008, and FY 2009, the number of hours of use of force training these trainees received as part of their overall basic training was consistent. Given the larger number of agents and officers trained, funding for use of force training at the Border Patrol Academy and the Field Operations Academy increased during those years. Tables 3 and 4 illustrate the number of trainee entrants and graduates, use of force training hours, and funding for use of force training for each basic academy for FY 2005–FY 2012.

Table 3: Border Patrol Academy Use of Force Training FY 2005–FY 2012

Fiscal Year	OBP Academy Trainee Entrants	OBP Academy Graduates	Use of Force Training Hours	Use of Force Training Funding
2005	926	734	126	$872,113
2006	1,889	1,408	126	$2,602,749
2007	3,912	3,060	124	$5,154,947
2008	4,566	3,323	124	$8,598,955
2009	4,861	3,582	124	$11,136,797
2010	1,578	1,250	124	$2,467,950
2011	1,745	1,394	134	$3,533,881
2012	735	629	134	$3,455,965

Source: CBP OBP and Office of Training and Development (OTD).

Table 4: Field Operations Academy Use of Force Training FY 2005–FY 2012

Fiscal Year	OFO Academy Trainee Entrants	OFO Academy Graduates	Use of Force Training Hours	Use of Force Training Funding
2005	1,286	1,188	155	$2,114,632
2006	1,368	1,232	156	$2,043,193
2007	2,064	1,841	156	$2,974,498
2008	2,823	2,563	154	$3,753,624
2009	3,090	2,914	154	$4,796,714
2010	142	117	208	$792,327
2011	546	515	212	$1,646,374
2012	1,229	1,156	212	$4,097,704

Source: CBP OFO and OTD.

Use of Force Training Post-Basic Quarterly Use of Force Training

Since October 2010, all CBP law enforcement agents and officers are required to qualify quarterly with their firearms and recertify annually with any less lethal devices they are certified to carry, such as a baton, pepper spray, or taser. To achieve these requirements, agents and officers complete at least 16 hours of firearms training and 16 hours of less lethal force training yearly, with 4 hours of each quarterly. Quarterly training includes—

1) Classroom instruction on either the firearm or a less lethal device as well as discussion of use of force policy and the use of force continuum;
2) A written exam;
3) Demonstration of proficiency with the firearm or less lethal device; and
4) Demonstration of appropriate judgment in training scenarios.

Prior to October 2010, CBP officers qualified only three times per year with their firearms. This requirement increased to quarterly with implementation of the unified CBP *Use of Force Handbook* in October 2010. A CBP official said the surge only improved training, resulting in more instructors and more training opportunities. For example, since 2010, all CBP officers become certified on the taser at their basic academy and must therefore recertify annually. Also, even though the workforce surge ended in 2009, the number of CBP agents and officers remains more than 43,000, so more agents and officers must complete quarterly training now and in the future, requiring more firearm and less lethal force instructors.

Instructor Training at CBP Advanced Training Center

Firearm instructors and less lethal force instructors complete instructor certification and recertification training at the CBP Advanced Training Center in Harpers Ferry, West Virginia. Certified instructors conduct quarterly use of force training for agents and officers in their areas of responsibility.

All instructors are trained based on the same standard regardless of whether they work for OBP, OFO, or the Office of Air and Marine (OAM). Firearm and less lethal force instructor trainees receive instruction on firearms or less lethal devices in addition to how to run proficiency drills. They also become proficient in developing, running, and debriefing training scenarios. Both firearm and less lethal force instructors must recertify every five years.

CBP Has Acted to Address Use of Force Incidents; More Can Be Done

CBP has taken several steps to address the number of use of force incidents. We also identified additional measures that CBP can take to address this issue. All CBP law enforcement agents and officers are required to follow a unified use of force policy, and CBP tracks all use of force incidents. Also, CBP conducted an internal review of use of force issues that resulted in several recommendations to improve use of force policies, training, equipment, tactics, and operational posture. In addition, the CBP Office of Training and Development (OTD) Use of Force Policy Division (UFPD) initiated a field audit program to assess the consistency of use of force training across CBP; however, formalization and expansion would improve the effectiveness of the program. Finally, CBP should continue to expand the use of scenario based training and evaluate new technologies to support agents and officers.

All CBP Law Enforcement Agents Required to Follow Unified Use of Force Policy

To establish common CBP requirements regarding use of force, all CBP law enforcement components have operated under a unified use of force policy since October 2010. Prior to this, each component operated under its separate pre DHS legacy use of force policy. Although the legacy policies had similarities, there were differences. For example, OBP agents qualified four times per year with their firearms, but OFO officers only qualified three times per year.

UFPD is responsible for developing all CBP use of force policy. To create the unified policy, representatives from each CBP component identified the best practices of each legacy policy and created a draft unified policy, and in 2007, CBP began negotiating with the bargaining units—the National Treasury

Employees Union and the National Border Patrol Council —the content of the proposed unified policy. CBP reached agreement with the unions in 2010; the unified policy then went to the CBP Commissioner for signature.

UFPD ensures that each CBP policy, directive, and procedure describing when and how CBP employees use force conforms to the CBP *Use of Force Policy Handbook*. UFPD also develops, maintains, and approves all CBP use of force training. Under the unified policy, all CBP agents and officers are trained to the same standard and receive the same amount of required use of force training every year. For example, all CBP officers and agents now receive eight hours of use of force training quarterly; training includes four hours of firearms training and four hours of less lethal force training each quarter. In addition, because all CBP instructors train to the same standard, use of force instructors from any CBP component can conduct use of force training for other CBP components. This provides CBP the ability to accommodate workforce surges or fill unexpected gaps.

UFPD Tracks All Uses of Force Involving CBP Employees; Additional Data Could Better Inform Analysis

To gain insight into use of force trends, training, and equipment needs, UFPD began tracking all use of force incidents involving CBP officers and agents in the Use of Force Reporting System (UFRS) in January 2010. Prior to 2010, only reports of serious use of force incidents were sent to the Commissioner's Situation Room. The UFRS tracks detailed information about uses of force involving CBP agents and officers; however, it does not track information regarding assaults on agents and officers that do not result in the use of force. Being able to incorporate information regarding assaults on Federal agents that do not result in the use of force directly from other CBP systems, such as the e3 Assault Module, would provide UFPD with more information on the threats agents face along the border and how they respond to those threats.

Incidents involving the use of deadly force or the use of less lethal devices must be reported to a supervisor within 1 hour of the incident and to UFRS within 72 hours. The involved agent or officer must provide information about the incident, including but not limited to the date, time, and location of the incident; the firearm(s) or device(s) used; the nature and extent of injuries or deaths; and descriptions of subjects involved or witnesses to the incident. A CBP supervisor enters incident information into UFRS for deadly force incidents, and the involved agent or officer or a CBP supervisor for incidents involving less lethal force. A CBP official said that information in UFRS is not used for discipline purposes. UFRS does not link to JICMS, and UFPD usually has no involvement in or knowledge of investigations of excessive force allegations.

UFPD analyzes the information in UFRS to determine whether to make changes to use of force policies, training, tactics, or equipment. The data can be viewed by CBP component, type of force used, type of weapon used, sector or field office, or region (southwest, northern, or coastal). For example, in FY 2011, agents and officers reported 1,188 uses of force in UFRS (see figure 3). Of the 1,188 uses of force, 1,029 (or 87 percent) were by OBP, 148 (or 12 percent) were by OFO, and 11 (or 1 percent) were by OAM. In FY 2012, agents and officers reported 936 uses of force in UFRS. Of these, 808 (or 86 percent) were by OBP, 96 (or 10 percent) were by OFO, 30 (or 3 percent) were by OAM, and 2 (or 0.2 percent) were by the Office of International Affairs.

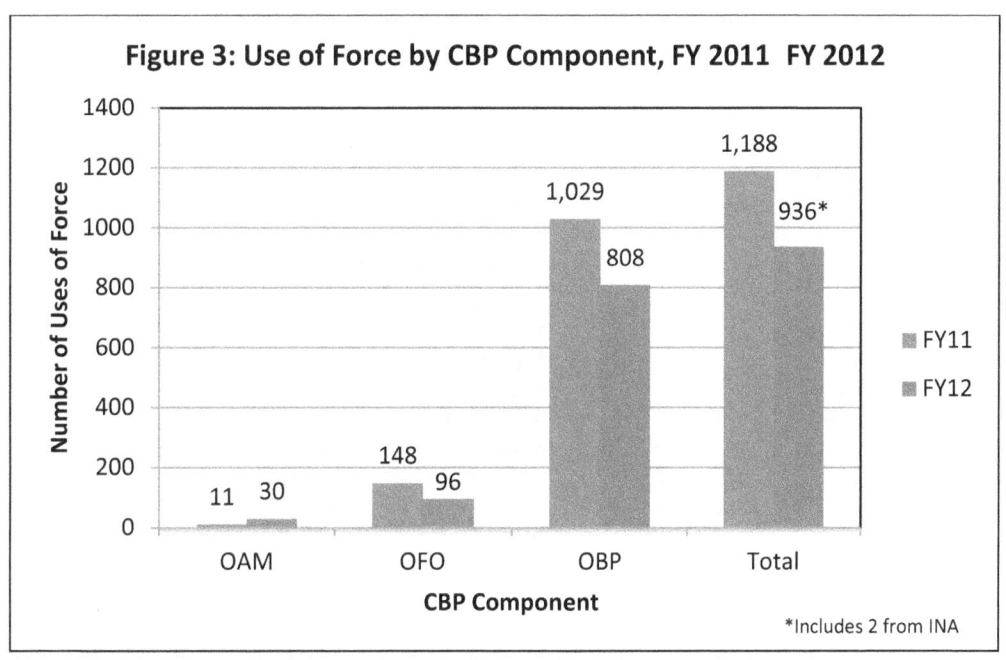

Figure 3: Use of Force by CBP Component, FY 2011 FY 2012

Source: CBP OTD UFPD.

Within CBP, 95 percent (1,133 of 1,188) of FY 2011 uses of force and 95 percent (885 of 936) of FY 2012 uses of force occurred along the southwest border of the United States. For OBP, 98 percent of FY 2011 uses of force and 98 percent of FY 2012 uses of force were along the southwest border. For OFO, 83 percent of FY 2011 uses of force and 89 percent of FY 2012 uses of force were along the southwest border.

When CBP agents and officers used force in FY 2011, they used firearms 7 percent of the time and less lethal force options 93 percent of the time. In FY

2012, they used firearms 6 percent of the time and less lethal force options 94 percent of the time. Within OBP, agents used firearms 7 percent of the time in FY 2011 and 7 percent of the time in FY 2012, less lethal force devices 84 percent and 82 percent of the time, respectively, and other force 9 percent and 12 percent of the time, respectively. For OFO, officers used firearms 7 percent and 2 percent of the time, respectively, in FY 2011 and FY 2012, less lethal force devices 78 percent and 96 percent of the time, and other force 15 percent and 2 percent of the time. Less lethal force devices include baton, pepper spray, taser, and other devices. Other force includes physical force without a weapon and the use of vehicles and canines. Figure 4 compares the types of force used by OBP and OFO during FY 2011 and FY 2012.

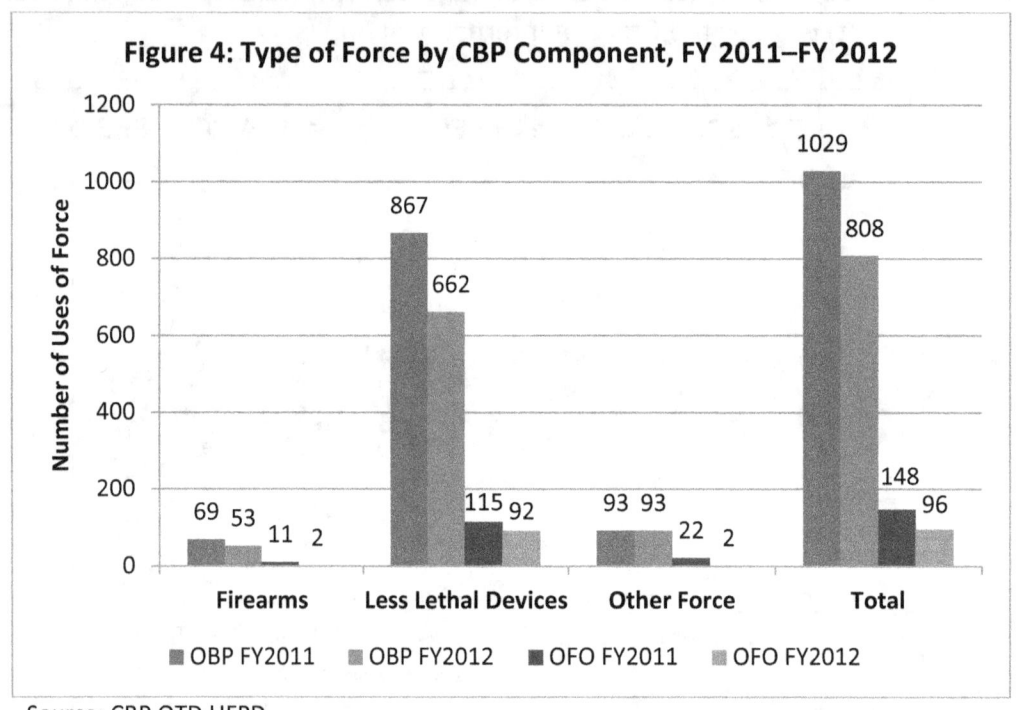

Figure 4: Type of Force by CBP Component, FY 2011–FY 2012

Source: CBP OTD UFPD.

Analysis of use of force data from UFRS provides UFPD with valuable information regarding the effectiveness of use of force policies, training, equipment, and tactics. However, including data from assaults on Federal agents that do not result in a use of force would provide additional valuable information. For example, rock attacks were the most frequent type of assault on agents in FY 2011 and the second most frequent type of assault in FY 2012. Of 339 reported rock assaults in FY 2011, agents did not respond with force to 188 (or 55 percent), responded with a firearm to 33 (or 10 percent), and used less lethal force in response to 118 (or 35 percent) of the rocking assaults, respectively. Of 185 rocking assaults in FY 2012, agents did not use force to respond to 121 (or 65 percent), responded with a firearm to 22 (or 12 percent), and used less lethal force in response to 42 (or 23 percent). Reviewing when force was used to respond to assaults as well as when agents did not respond with force could inform UFPD policy, guidance, equipment, and tactics regarding use of force in response to rocking or other types of assaults.

All uses of force must be reported by the employee or a supervisor in the UFRS, and all assaults on Federal agents must be reported in the e3 Assault Module. If an agent is assaulted and responds using any type of force, the incident would be reported in both systems. However, assaults that do not lead to a use of force response would be reported only in the e3 Assault Module. Knowing when agents do not respond with force when assaulted and which types of force are used in response to different types of assaults, in addition to use of force information from UFRS, would provide a clearer operational picture for CBP management. In addition, it could identify best practices, especially regarding de escalation of potential use of force situations and provide insight into specific types of threats, such as rockings, that place agents in potential use of force situations. Also, UFPD would have additional information to improve training, tactics, equipment, and policies involving use of force. UFPD should develop a process to incorporate information regarding assaults on agents that do not result in the use of force into its analysis of use of force incidents.

In addition, when an assault on an agent results in the use of force and must be reported in both UFRS and the e3 Assault Module, similar information is collected about the assault in both systems. A CBP official suggested creating a link between the two systems to facilitate entering the information and ensure reports are made in both systems when necessary. Developing a link between the systems could remind agents to complete reports in both places when appropriate and could ensure that assault information required by both systems is entered consistently. Also, it could facilitate the incorporation of non response assault data into use of force incident analysis.

Recommendation

We recommend that U.S. Customs and Border Protection:

Recommendation #2:

Develop a process to incorporate information regarding assaults on agents that did not result in agents using force into its analysis of use of force incidents.

CBP Initiated Internal Review of Use of Force Issues

Following several deadly force incidents, CBP initiated its own internal review of use of force issues in November 2012. The review included three parts—field reviews of select incidents by the CBP Use of Force Incident Review Team, reviews of 67 shooting incidents by the Use of Force Incident Review Committee, and an external review of the 67 incidents and CBP use of force policies by the Police Executive Research Forum. The review focused on the effectiveness of current use of force policies, equipment, tactics, training, and operational posture. CBP's review made ▮ recommendations, and PERF's review made ▮, to ▮▮▮▮▮▮▮▮

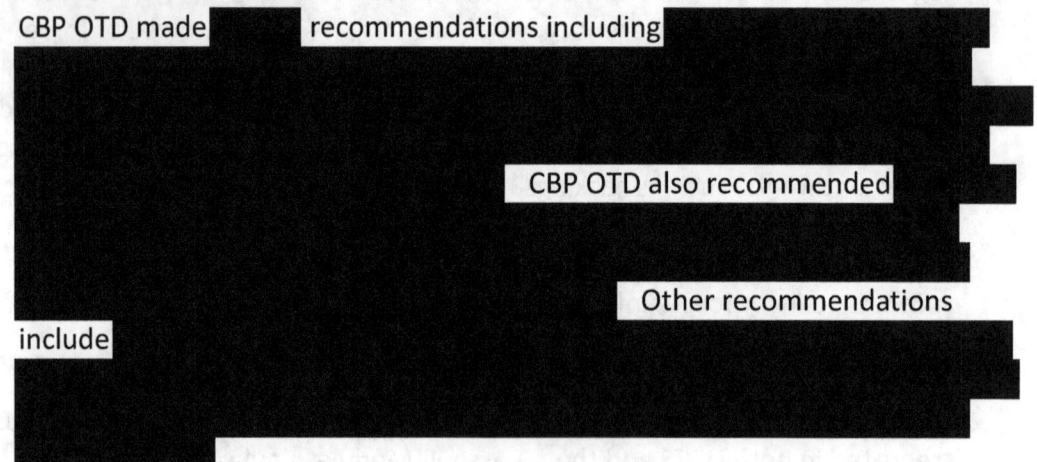

CBP OTD made ▮▮▮▮ recommendations including ▮▮▮▮▮▮▮

CBP OTD also recommended ▮▮▮▮

Other recommendations include ▮▮▮▮.

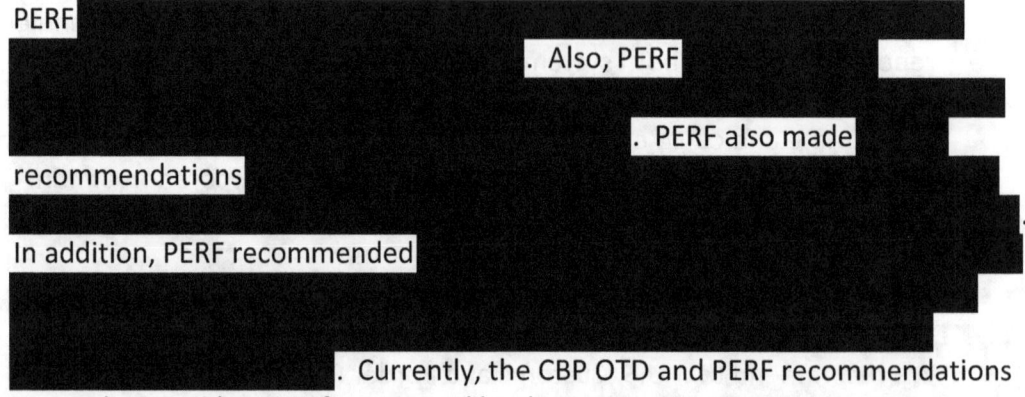

PERF ▮▮▮▮. Also, PERF ▮▮▮▮. PERF also made ▮▮▮▮ recommendations ▮▮▮▮

In addition, PERF recommended ▮▮▮▮. Currently, the CBP OTD and PERF recommendations are under consideration for approval by the Acting CBP Commissioner.

UFPD Initiated Field Audit Program; Needs More Formalization and Expansion

In FY 2012, UFPD implemented a field audit program to assess use of force training. The program determines whether training is consistent with CBP policy, instructor guidebooks and lesson plans, and the intent of the less lethal force and firearms training programs, as well as whether safety protocols are followed. Each field audit may result in recommendations for corrective action to both the Office of Training and Development and the audited field location. While the UFPD field audit program is a good first step for UFPD management to assess whether use of force training in the field is consistent with use of force policy, there is no formal process for recommendation followup, no system to assess results and make appropriate timely changes to use of force training, and not enough program staff.

When conducting a field audit, three person teams from UFPD spend three days at each location observing quarterly firearms and less lethal force training and identifying strengths, weaknesses, and necessary changes. The audit team provides oral feedback to instructors and training coordinators at each location to correct issues observed during the audit. Following the field audit, the team lead prepares a report including recommendations for corrective actions. UFPD sends the report to the audited location and follows up by telephone with the inspected office to discuss planned actions for addressing recommendations.

We observed a field audit team conduct a field audit in February 2013. At that time, only one agent was dedicated full time to the UFPD field audit program. A senior CBP official said that additional staff would strengthen the field audit program.

UFPD identified several major issues during its 2012 field audits. For example, some locations were not getting the full number of required training hours, were not giving written tests during less lethal force recertification training, or were not using the correct course of fire for firearms qualifications. UFPD advised instructors and training coordinators at respective locations to correct specific issues. Issues observed at one location are typically corrected only at that location because there is no formal process to evaluate audit results.

The UFPD field audit team observed that many agents and officers do not understand use of force and the extent to which they may or may not use force. The field audit team recommended to OTD   and suggested that

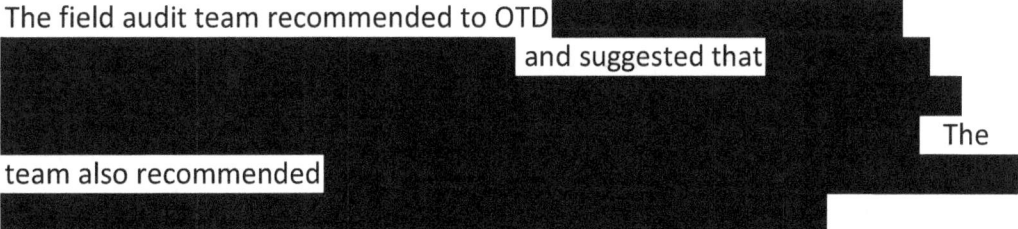

team also recommended

CBP has noted in its formal comments that, of the 32 field training reviews conducted to date, this was observed only once, at one location and involved a small number of agents on one training day.

Developing a process to identify this type of issue, implement changes into use of force training, and disseminate them to the field would improve consistency and standardization regarding use of force across CBP. Formalizing and expanding the field audit program will require additional staff.

Recommendation

We recommend that U.S. Customs and Border Protection:

Recommendation #3:

Develop a formal process to evaluate use of force training field audit results and follow up on field audit recommendations.

CBP Should Continue To Expand Use of Scenario-based Training

Scenario based training provides agents and officers the opportunity for hands on practice. Training scenarios reinforce classroom instruction regarding use of force policy, tactics, and justifications. Within the safety of a training environment, they experience realistic situations in which they must decide whether to use force and at what level, and then justify their actions. To ensure that agents and officers are sufficiently trained to confront threats, CBP should continue to expand scenario based training, including developing scenarios around high risk threats such as vehicular and rock assaults, adding training in low light conditions, and creating new realistic training environments.

Training scenarios allow agents to practice making appropriate use of force judgments as they handle the situation. They also learn the importance of and practice articulating their response to the situation and justification for the level of force used. In addition, instructors emphasize that choosing appropriate tactics initially can de escalate the situation and stop it from becoming a deadly force incident. Successfully completing a scenario creates an experience memory that could be useful should a similar "real life" situation arise.

Less lethal force and firearms instructors learn how to create, run, and debrief training scenarios during instructor certification courses at the CBP Advanced Training Center. They are encouraged to create training scenarios that represent realistic situations agents could encounter in their specific locations. Possible scenarios could include a single agent while on patrol encountering a large group of illegal aliens, responding to a report of people climbing the border fence, or responding to a port of entry regarding a car with a license plate matching a lookout notice.

CBP is assessing ways to improve use of force training. To provide a new and more realistic southwest border training environment, CBP plans to build a mock international border fence training area at both the CBP Advanced Training Center and the Border Patrol Academy. This would enable CBP to conduct scenario based training in a realistic field environment that many agents encounter during their careers. CBP has the materials needed to build the border fence training areas; however, due to budget constraints, CBP is reassessing when to build the fences.

During its internal review of use of force issues, UFPD determined that CBP basic academies do not train new agents and officers on all less lethal options that will be available to them. UFPD also identified high risk situations, such as vehicular and rock assaults, that are not sufficiently trained at the basic academies.

In addition, several officials said the use of scenario based training should be increased during basic training, especially at the Border Patrol Academy. They said trainees leave the Border Patrol Academy with the necessary tools and tactics, but are not fully prepared for possible real life situations they might encounter. For example, one official said trainees do not have the opportunity in a training environment to experience how they might react in an encounter in the field and practice working through their stress or fear reaction. CBP officials said that by experiencing possible scenarios and reactions in a training environment, trainees are better prepared for any situation they encounter in the field. We agree with suggestions to increase scenario based training at the basic academies.

CBP Assesses New Technology To Ensure Field Agents Have the Right Tools

CBP continuously assesses new lethal and less lethal equipment technology, tactics, and training to ensure that agents and officers have the skills and tools when needed. Currently, UFPD officials are emphasizing less lethal tools and trying to increase safety for both the agents and subjects involved in encounters that result in agent's use of force. In addition, officials are assessing training environments and adding simulator equipment to improve the effectiveness and consistency of use of force training across CBP.

Given different operational environments along the border, CBP has made multiple less lethal options available to agents. For example, there are several different less lethal devices that will deploy pepper spray or pepper ball chemicals to immobilize subjects. These tools are effective from varying distances and some deploy straight whereas others are able to arc over objects. Devices capable of arcing are more effective in border areas separated by a border fence, and devices that do not arc would be effective along areas of the border separated by river or where there are no line of sight obstacles. CBP is assessing other less lethal options that would allow an agent to deploy a less lethal device effectively from a greater distance.

Finally, CBP is evaluating the use of simulators, which can encompass all of use of force training, including training scenarios and firearms targeting and marksmanship. Using simulators for some scenario based training would allow an instructor to freeze an ongoing scenario to allow an agent to review or discuss policy or the agent's action at specific decision points in the scenario as well as recording and replaying the agent's actions during the post scenario debrief. In addition, because UFPD identifies use of force trends, incorporating simulators into use of force training would allow UFPD to create scenarios at the Advanced Training Center and disseminate them for use in the field. While field instructors would continue to develop location specific live scenarios, adding UFPD created training scenarios, especially in simulators, would reinforce standardization and consistency across CBP. It would also allow UFPD to create a scenario based on recent trends and implement it in the field quickly.

CBP is moving forward to incorporate simulator training as part of use of force training. After observing demonstrations of several different simulators on the market, UFPD officials selected several for in depth testing at the Advanced Training Center. In the current testing phase, UFPD officials set up each simulator at the Advanced Training Center, learn how to run the systems, and practice with each to determine its benefits, drawbacks, and how it could support CBP training needs. During the testing, UFPD officials are prioritizing requirements for the simulator system CBP will acquire. UFPD officials hope to acquire one simulator for the CBP Advanced Training Center and incorporate it into training classes by the end of FY 2013. Officials expect to spend about six months creating scenarios, running students through scenarios, and assessing the effectiveness of the simulator before placing simulators in the field. We observed instructor led scenario based training and demonstrations of two simulators. We concluded that the simulator has the potential to enhance the quality of CBP agent and officer training.

Polygraphs Improve Quality of Workforce

In 2008, CBP Internal Affairs began implementing a requirement that CBP conduct polygraph examinations of all prospective CBP law enforcement agents and officers by January 2013. When CBP began the polygraph program, approximately half of prospective agents or officers failed the examination. According to one CBP official, polygraphing 100 percent of prospective law enforcement agents and officers identifies and eliminates applicants who should not be in law enforcement. Pre employment polygraphs have improved the quality of the workforce. CBP Internal Affairs implemented the mandate well before the deadline and has been polygraphing 100 percent of law enforcement applicants since mid 2012.

Management Comments and OIG Analysis

We evaluated the formal comments CBP submitted and have made changes to the report where we deemed appropriate. A summary of the CBP response to each recommendation, and our analysis, is included below. A copy of the CBP response, in its entirety, appears in appendix B. In addition, we received technical comments from CBP and the DHS Office for Civil Rights and Civil Liberties and incorporated these comments into the report where appropriate. CBP concurred with all recommendations in the report.

Recommendation 1: Work with ICE to implement a method in JICMS to identify each use of force allegation involving an officer or agent.

Management Response: CBP concurs. The CBP Office of Internal Affairs, in collaboration with the CBP Office of Training and Development (OTD)/Use of Force Policy Division (UFPD) and Immigration and Customs Enforcement (ICE)/Office of Professional Responsibility, are developing a "menu" of categories in the Joint Integrity Case Management System (JICMS) to help identify each use of force incident or allegation involving an officer or agent.

OIG Analysis: The actions planned by ICE and CBP appear to be consistent with the intent of the recommendation. Only when we examine the new JICMS structure will we be able to determine if compliance has been achieved. We consider recommendation 1 Resolved Open.

Recommendation 2: Develop a process to incorporate information regarding assaults on agents that did not result in agents using force into its analysis of use of force incidents.

Management Response: CBP concurs. The addition of assault data where force was not used by the officer/agent will provide a baseline to compare with incidents where force was used by the officer/agent. This data will provide a broader understanding of how use of force decisions are being made as well as the effectiveness of use of force training and policy. OTD/UFPD will work closely with other CBP offices to use and cross reference this information. Initially, CBP will coordinate internally to ensure the owners of the different assault data collection systems and the Use of Force Reporting System share and analyze data. Long term, CBP will link these systems electronically so that this data is easily accessible and may be used to provide comprehensive use of force analysis to include assaults that did not result in a use of force by a CBP agent or officer. CBP will have internal coordination between system owners in place by the end of the first quarter, Fiscal Year 2014 (FY14) and, barring any delays caused by limited resources, will have the systems connected electronically by the end of FY14.

OIG Analysis: The actions planned by CBP appear to be consistent with the intent of the recommendation. Only when we examine the results of the CBP process modifications will we be able to determine if compliance has been achieved. We consider recommendation 2 Resolved Open.

Recommendation 3: Develop a formal process to evaluate use of force training field audit results and follow up on field audit recommendations.

Management Response: CBP concurs. OTD/UFPD has conducted field training reviews at 32 locations since February 2012. Although a relatively new practice, these reviews have been extremely effective in identifying strengths, weaknesses, best practices, and providing general oversight of CBP's use of force training. The program was a proactive step implemented by CBP to improve field training, and we agree that further expansion of the program will only improve it. CBP is updating Use of Force policy to institutionalize the formal process governing use of force training reviews. CBP is developing and formalizing a Standard Operating Procedure that provides guidance for evaluating field review results and implementing review recommendations. An initial draft of the Standard Operating Procedure will be completed by the end of the 2nd quarter FY14. In addition, CBP is developing the capability to conduct more comprehensive quantitative and qualitative analyses of use of force incident reviews with the establishment of the Use of Force Center of Excellence (UFCE). Barring any delays caused by limited resources, CBP expects to have the UFCE established and this capability operational during FY14.

OIG Analysis: The actions planned by CBP appear to be consistent with the intent of the recommendation. We will we determine if compliance has been achieved after reviewing the results of the CBP program changes. We consider recommendation 3 Resolved Open.

Appendix A
Objectives, Scope, and Methodology

The Department of Homeland Security (DHS) Office of Inspector General (OIG) was established by the *Homeland Security Act of 2002* (Public Law 107 296) by amendment to the *Inspector General Act of 1978*. This is one of a series of audit, inspection, and special reports prepared as part of our oversight responsibilities to promote economy, efficiency, and effectiveness within the Department.

In May 2012, Senator Robert Menendez and 15 members of Congress asked that we review incidents involving the use of force by CBP employees. Specifically, our objectives were to (1) examine and summarize reports of investigation alleging brutality and use of excessive force by CBP employees, (2) determine what reforms DHS has implemented to address the number of incidents involving the use of force by CBP employees, and (3) determine what effect adding more agents and officers to the workforce has had on training and professionalism.

We conducted our fieldwork between September 2012 and April 2013. We reviewed current and former use of force policies, directives, and handbooks; use of force training curricula, guidebooks, schedules, and funding; and three OIG reports of investigation. In addition, we reviewed and analyzed data on excessive force and abuse allegations and investigations, intentional discharges of a weapon, staffing numbers of CBP agents and officers, use of force incidents within CBP, deadly force incidents within CBP, assaults on Border Patrol Agents, and numbers of OBP and OFO basic academy trainees and graduates. We also reviewed UFPD field audit reports, CBP use of force self inspection records, and the results of a CBP internal review of use of force issues that included an external assessment of significant use of force shooting incidents by the Police Executive Research Forum.

We conducted 40 meetings with 85 officials within DHS, CBP, the Department of Justice, the Mexican Embassy, and nongovernmental organizations. We visited the CBP Advanced Training Center in Harpers Ferry, West Virginia, four times to observe less lethal force and firearms use of force training and equipment. We also conducted a site visit to San Diego, California. During our site visit, we met with OBP officials and observed a UFPD field audit team conducting an audit of OBP and OFO use of force training.

We conducted this review under the authority of the *Inspector General Act of 1978*, as amended, and according to the Quality Standards for Inspections issued by the Council of the Inspectors General on Integrity and Efficiency.

Appendix B
Management Comments to the Draft Report

1300 Pennsylvania Avenue NW
Washington, DC 20229

**U.S. Customs and
Border Protection**

August 9, 2013

MEMORANDUM FOR:	Charles. K. Edwards Deputy Inspector General Department of Homeland Security
FROM:	Assistant Commissioner, Office of Internal Affairs U.S. Customs and Border Protection
SUBJECT:	Response to the Office of Inspector General's Draft Report *"CBP Use of Force Training and Actions to Address Use of Force Incidents"*

Thank you for the opportunity to review and provide comment on this draft report entitled, *"CBP Use of Force Training and Actions to Address Use of Force Incidents" (OIG-12-160-ISP-CBP).*

U.S. Customs and Border Protection (CBP) appreciates the acknowledgement of CBP's continued commitment to our workforce. As highlighted in the report, CBP's workforce surge did not affect use of force training but in fact, training remained consistent. Also, the implementation of the polygraph examinations for all prospective law enforcement agents and officers has improved the quality of the CBP workforce by detecting unsuitable candidates. The report also recognizes the steps taken by CBP to address use of force incidents involving CBP employees, for instance: (1) completing an internal review of use of force issues; (2) beginning the tracking of all use of force incidents; (3) improving consistency in training for agents and officers, and the application of use of force standards and policies; and (4) initiating a field audit program to evaluate training across CBP field locations.

The report mentions a number of agents and officers were unfamiliar with the use of force policy and the extent to which they may use force. CBP would like to note, of the 32 field training reviews conducted to date, this was observed only once, at one location and involved a small number of agents on one training day. In that instance, field review team personnel took immediate action with the field instructors to address the problem and later followed up with a written after action report and verbal discussions with that location's training personnel. This case illustrates the value and effectiveness of these field reviews.

The draft report contains three recommendations directed to CBP, with which we concur. Specifically, OIG recommended that:

Recommendation 1: Work with ICE to implement a method in JICMS to identify each use of force allegation involving an officer or agent.

Response: CBP concurs. The CBP Office of Internal Affairs, in collaboration with the CBP Office of Training and Development (OTD)/Use of Force Policy Division (UFPD) and Immigration and Customs Enforcement (ICE)/Office of Professional Responsibility, are developing a "menu" of categories in the Joint Integrity Case Management System (JICMS) to help identify each use of force incident or allegation involving an officer or agent. CBP and ICE are looking at a tentative JICMS release date of August 24, 2013.

Recommendation 2: Develop a process to incorporate information regarding assaults on agents that did not result in agents using force into its analysis of use of force incidents.

Response: CBP concurs. The addition of assault data where force was not used by the officer/agent will provide a baseline to compare with incidents where force was used by the officer/agent. This will provide a broader understanding of how use of force decisions are being made in the field as well as the effectiveness of use of force training and policy. The OTD/UFPD will work closely with other CBP offices to utilize and cross-reference this information.

Initially, CBP will coordinate internally to ensure the owners of the different assault data collection systems and the Use of Force Reporting System share and analyze data. Long term, CBP will link these systems electronically so that this data is easily accessible and may be used to provide comprehensive use of force analysis to include assaults that did not result in a use of force by a CBP agent or officer. CBP will have internal coordination between system owners in place by the end of the first quarter, Fiscal Year 2014 (FY14) and, barring any delays caused by limited resources, will have the systems connected electronically by the end of FY14.

Recommendation 3: Develop a formal process to evaluate use of force training field audit results and follow up on field audit recommendations.

Response: CBP concurs. The OTD/UFPD has conducted field training reviews at 32 locations since February 2012. Although a relatively new practice, these reviews have been extremely effective in identifying strengths, weaknesses, best practices, and providing general oversight of CBP's use of force training. The program was a proactive step implemented by CBP to improve field training and we agree that further expansion of the program will only improve it.

CBP is updating Use of Force policy to institutionalize the formal process governing use of force training reviews. CBP is developing and formalizing a Standard Operating Procedure that provides guidance for evaluating field review results and implementing review recommendations. An initial draft of the Standard Operating Procedure will be completed by the end of the 2nd quarter FY14. In addition, CBP is developing the capability to conduct more robust quantitative and qualitative analysis of use of force incident reviews with the establishment of the Use of Force Center of Excellence (UFCE). Barring any delays caused by limited resources, CBP expects to have the UFCE established and this capability operational during FY14.

Although not specified as formal recommendations, we also agree with the OIG's recommendation that we should continue to expand the use of scenario-based training and continue to pursue new technologies to ensure field agents have the right skills and tools when needed.

CBP is committed to the continual improvement of our use of force programs, and will work with our internal components and DHS partners to implement the recommendations.

Appendix C
Major Contributors to This Report

William McCarron, Chief Inspector
Douglas Ellice, Chief Inspector
Jennifer A. Lindsey, Lead Inspector
Tanya Suggs, Inspector
Anne Cho, Inspector
Ryan P. Cassidy, Inspector

Appendix D
Report Distribution

Department of Homeland Security

Secretary
Deputy Secretary
Chief of Staff
Deputy Chief of Staff
General Counsel
Executive Secretary
Director, GAO/OIG Liaison Office
Assistant Secretary for Office of Policy
Assistant Secretary for Office of Public Affairs
Assistant Secretary for Office of Legislative Affairs
CBP Liaison
Acting Chief Privacy Officer

Office of Management and Budget

Chief, Homeland Security Branch
DHS OIG Budget Examiner

Congress

Congressional Oversight and Appropriations Committees, as appropriate